"On May 9, 1971, Johnny Cash sat in a pew of a small Pentecostal church just outside Nashville. The preacher finished his sermon and began to make an altar call, appealing to the congregation to come down front and make things right with God.

"Johnny Cash stood up, stepped into the aisle, and walked a few short steps to the wooden altar. He knelt heavily on the deep-red carpet and, in his own words, 'made a complete dedication of my life to Jesus Christ.'

" '. . . I've lived all my life for the devil up 'til now, and from here on I'm going to live it for the Lord.' "

The New
JOHNNY
CASH

CHARLES PAUL CONN

SPIRE BOOKS

Old Tappan, New Jersey

Photographs from *The Gospel Road*
courtesy of 20th Century-Fox Film Corporation.

*Scripture quotations in this volume are from the King
James Version of the Bible.*

THE NEW JOHNNY CASH

A SPIRE BOOK
Published by Pyramid Publications for
Fleming H. Revell Company

Spire edition published November, 1973
    Third printing January, 1974

Copyright © 1973 by Fleming H. Revell Company
All Rights Reserved

Library of Congress Catalog Card Number: 73-2381

ISBN: 0-8007-0607-2

Printed in the United States of America

SPIRE BOOKS are published by Fleming H. Revell Company
Old Tappan, New Jersey 07675, U.S.A.

...if any man be in Christ,
   he is a new creature:
   old things are passed away;
behold, all things are become new.

2 Corinthians 5:17

The New
Johnny
Cash

1

IT WAS A WEEKDAY IN ATLANTA, AND the coach section of the airliner was packed with middle-aged passengers, most of them wearing business suits and dour, tired expressions that seemed appropriately gray in the haze of cigarette smoke they poured into the air.

Just before the door was pulled shut a bright, blond, college girl burst through the opening and into the plane. Her clothes and her smile and the way she bounced into the cabin and into her seat all matched perfectly: she was happy, infectiously and irresistibly happy, and she brightened up the cabin of the plane just by walking through the door.

Her seat was between two businessmen types, and as she wriggled into place they almost involuntarily pulled their magazines down from around their faces and prepared for conversation. They weren't disappointed. Her name was Gwen. She was a student from North Carolina, she said. And she was on her way home from Explo '72 in Dallas, she said. And she was learning how great it was to be a Christian for the first time in her life and had met lots of exciting people in Dallas and had never dreamed there were so many young Christians in the country.

"I was in Dallas four days," she continued, "and there were hundreds of thousands of people. We had these big rallies in the Cotton Bowl, and there wasn't even enough room for all the people in *there*. And then at the very end of the convention, there was a big Christian-music festival. They blocked off a highway and everybody sat right on the ground. It was unreal! All kinds of people sang —some of these new gospel-rock groups and some religious quartets and all kinds of people.

"I guess the guy that really zonked me out the most was Johnny Cash. He was there with his whole group and sang right before Billy Graham preached. Man, Cash was really something! He told how much it meant to him to be a Christian, and quoted Scripture verses between songs. When he sang, he got that whole place to jumping!"

A puzzled look tugged momentarily at her face, and she went on, "Come to think of it, I never have thought of Johnny Cash as a Christian before. Isn't he supposed to be a pretty rough guy? I mean, back a few years ago, didn't he drink a lot or do dope or something?"

Yes, Gwen, Johnny Cash drank or did dope or something. Yes, indeed, he was supposed to be a pretty rough guy. And those tales you remember hearing about him—well, some of them are true and some of them probably are not.

But the Johnny Cash of 1973 is greatly different from the Cash of the 1960s, whose career was a jagged line of brilliance and tragedy, his legendary magnetism on stage always playing to the counterpoint of broken concert dates, drug arrests, and the constant theme of tragedy and self-destruction in his life. And he is also different—less dramatically so, perhaps, but different nonetheless—from the TV star of three or four years ago, the "rehabilitated" Johnny Cash who became the most sought-after entertainer ever to emerge from the Nashville world of country-western music.

The difference between the Cash of then and the Cash of now is due to a religious change, a gradual transformation from an apparently irreligious man to one who is, by any yardstick, deeply and permanently committed to personal discipleship with Jesus Christ.

As a celebrity who lives under the daily scrutiny of the public eye, Cash has been unable to experience that transformation with any privacy—that is an obscurity which can be enjoyed only by less well-known men. His behavior and conversation have been watched by a curious and not-always-understanding public every step of the way. And so it happens that one of the most powerful testimonies of spiritual renewal in this generation has been played out on center stage, with a secular press, often insensitive to the dynamics of Cash's growing relationship with God, documenting the unfolding story.

There are those around Cash, including those who know him best, who will tell you that Cash has not changed at all, that at heart he has always been a deeply religious person, and his "change" over the past few years has been merely a return to what has always been basic and essential to him. Perhaps they are right. But the vibrations that he sends out when he talks and sings today testify to something of much greater substance than merely the personality of a good and decent man. They speak of personal, vibrant acquaintance with a living Christ, and of a single-minded absorption in the work of His kingdom. That is the *new* Johnny Cash.

The time will likely come when Cash will tell the story for himself. When he does, it will be a story that will excite and enrich every Christian who hears it, and one that will nudge unbelievers closer to their own confrontations with God and themselves. What follows is not that inside story. It does not pretend to be. It is, rather, an unadorned report on the making of the new Johnny Cash. It is the simple, straightforward account of a complex, richly talented man who has emerged from a life of constant crisis to become a servant of God.

2

IT WOULD BE DIFFICULT TO LIVE IN
America in the 1960s and '70s and not know about
Johnny Cash. All the standard show business
clichés were long ago worn out on him by the writ-
ers of the entertainment world.

He is a superstar of the first and brightest mag-
nitude. Since 1956, when his recording of "I Walk
the Line" was the top popular song of the year,
Cash has reigned as the unchallenged "king of the
hill" among country-western musicians. He has
written or recorded literally dozens of hits, among
them "Ring of Fire," "Folsom Prison Blues," "A
Boy Named Sue," and "Jackson," the Grammy
Award winning duet recorded with his wife June

Carter. The walls of his offices are solid with gold records, awards, and tributes of every description.

Though his career began on the country-western circuit, and he still identifies strongly with that segment of the entertainment industry, Cash's greatest uniqueness has been his ability to appeal effectively to a transcultural American audience. He is not a "country" singer in the traditional sense, nor can he be called "folk" or "rock" or "pop," nor stuffed into any other of the stereotyped categories by which most performers are described. His appeal is universal, and no segment of the population is immune to his special kind of charisma:

• He is lionized by the followers of traditional country music. Since he sang as a regular on the "Grand Ole Opry," he has been the single most sought-after performer of that genre, and still electrifies "Grand Ole Opry" crowds with his occasional guest appearances there.

• The often-hypercritical teen and college crowds hail him as one of the few "genuine" personalities on the show-business scene and are drawn to his style for its simplicity and authentic earthiness.

• He is respected enough by folk-music purists to rate an invitation to the Newport Folk Festival in Rhode Island, and to receive rave reviews for his performance there.

• In the all-inclusive category of popular music (disc jockeys call it "middle-of-road"), he has had a consistent output of hits and record sales that only singers of Sinatra-Presley-Tom Jones status have matched. His prime-time TV show ran for three successful seasons through 1971, the final proof that he has "arrived" as a superstar of national eminence who is not limited by the tastes of any single type of musical audience.

The career of Johnny Cash began in a way not unlike that of thousands more who have tried and failed. A native of Dyess, Arkansas, he grew up to the music of Hank Williams and Jimmie Rodgers, and the songs of the fundamentalist church and the "Grand Ole Opry" were mixed and mingled in a musical backdrop that was always a part of him.

Cash left the farmland of Arkansas as a teenager for a job in the up-north city of Detroit, but he was unhappy and out-of-sorts there. He returned home, joined the Air Force just as the Korean War broke out, and soon found himself doing a tour of duty as a radio operator in Landsberg, Germany.

It was there that Cash learned two things that were to figure importantly in his future: He learned to play the guitar, and he learned to like the taste of liquor.

It was the early fifties, the height of the United States–Soviet Union cold war in Europe, and Cash was assigned the nerve-scraping job of intercepting and copying Soviet radio messages. He was extremely good at the job and the demands on his time and energy in critical periods of United States–Soviet military gamesmanship were enormous. To ease the tension of that responsibility and to fill the loneliness of off-duty hours so far from home, Cash turned to music as if it were salvation itself.

He made close friends—most of them country boys like himself—and the commonality around which their comradeship flourished was the music they had all loved back home. One of his buddies taught Cash to play the guitar, and soon he bought his own cheap six-string model and was strummin' and pickin' in earnest.

He was then, as now, moody and introspective, a private person in the best sense of the phrase; and he found that he could express himself, and amuse himself, with a guitar and a quiet place to fondle it and learn to know it better. He began to make up his own tunes, write lines and lyrics that said what he wanted to say better than the songs that were already packaged and worn.

Cash was discharged in 1954, and almost immediately married Vivian Liberto, a San Antonio brunette whom he had met three years earlier at Lackland Air Force Base. By this time he was serious about trying to break into music, and moved with his new wife to Memphis, Tennessee, where he worked as an appliance salesman, often selling door-to-door, and attended radio announcer's school part-time.

It was there, struggling to make ends meet from week to week, that Cash met Marshall Grant and Luther Perkins. Both were mechanics at a local garage, and both, like Cash, were devoted (if amateurish) country-music buffs. They were hooked on the soft sound of an acoustical guitar, the thump of a bass, the plaintive melodies and lyrics of down-home music. With the financial backing of Cash's appliance-store boss, the three started a fifteen-minute radio broadcast of gospel music that aired every Saturday afternoon. The show lasted only two months, but by the time those months were over, the morale and confidence of the three was soaring, and they decided to try for a recording audition—maybe they could cut a gospel record at Sun Records, then a small studio in Memphis.

The gospel album didn't work out (not interested, said the studio after listening to the group's repertoire), but studio director Sam Phillips liked what he heard enough to suggest they try again with a country-rock song. A few months later, they got their chance, and cut a single with "Hey, Porter" on one side and "Cry, Cry, Cry" on the other. Both were Cash's songs, and when the record was finally released it sold over one hundred thousand copies. That was the storybook beginning of Johnny Cash and the Tennessee Two, and it was promising enough for the trio eventually to quit their jobs and take a fling at the big time. With Cash growling into the microphone and Grant and Perkins rooting out the notes on an old, upright bass and an electric guitar, they went on the road.

After a second single broke onto the national charts, the trio got an offer to sing on the "Louisiana Hayride," a country radio program which was broadcast live out of Shreveport, Louisiana, in much the same way that the "Grand Ole Opry" is aired before a live audience from Nashville. Like the "Opry," the "Hayride" was a Saturday-night show, and by the time the group arrived back in Memphis early Sunday morning, they were carrying with them a contract to appear as regulars on the show every weekend.

The road from there to the top was straight-up and wide-open, and Johnny Cash and the Tennessee Two traveled it at breakneck speed, hitting every bump and pothole along the way. Turning their schedule management over to Bob Neal (a disc jockey-turned-agent who was also managing Elvis Presley at the time), they found themselves furiously busy on the country-music circuit, singing one-nighters almost daily in towns which were somtimes hundreds of miles apart. They drove an old Plymouth that ran well, poorly, or not at all, depending on its own unpredictable whim. Pay was barely enough to be called a living wage. Meals were skimpy and spasmodic. Dressing rooms and motels were third-rate or nonexistent. But it was show business, and Cash seemed to thrive on it. By now he was gaining a bit of public visibility that might even be described as fame. The crowds were boisterously receptive to the rough, hard-driving style of the group. And Cash was learning to write country songs—good, marketable songs—with a skill and sensitivity that even now he is hard-pressed to beat.

One such song was a simple, understated tune called "I Walk the Line." Released in 1956 by Sun Records, it was a blockbuster. In those days, the line between country and pop music was much more severely drawn than now. (Cash, in fact, is one of the primary forces that pulled the two together.) It was practically unthinkable for a release that was branded "country-western" to make a significant dent on the best-seller charts among pop records. Country music was still painfully unfashionable in 1956, and the dramatic success of "I Walk the Line" in both markets was a precedent-shattering accomplishment.

Many people feel that "I Walk the Line" is still the most memorable of the many songs from Cash's pen. Apparently he agrees. The wall of his personal office at the House of Cash complex is adorned with a gigantic copy of the score of the tune. It dominates the room, and seems to testify to his gratitude for the role it played in catapulting him so suddenly into national prominence.

The song zoomed to the number-one position on both pop music and country-music charts, held that spot for forty-four consecutive weeks, and sold nearly two million copies. By the time the record finally peaked, Cash was a nationally famous performer, unquestionably the top country singer in the land, and was building for himself an audience of loyalists who would never forget who he was. He signed a recording contract with Columbia Records, moved his wife and three daughters to a new home in California (more and more of his concerts were there now), and began to squeeze the entertainment business for all the money and all the excitement that it offered country music's hottest property. By 1960 Cash was making a quarter of a million dollars a year. He was on the way.

The next part of the Johnny Cash story is a crazy tale of a man simultaneously on his way up and on his way down.

Professionally, things kept getting better and better. In his personal life, they got worse and worse, and finally began to fall apart.

The only thing wrong with being rich, famous, and in demand was the pace it created. Suddenly Cash was pulling down big money by the double fistfulls, with personal appearances all over the world, recording sessions as frequent as the market would allow, and a non-stop ticket to exhaustion. He was a big man, a healthy man, but the drain on his energy was endless, and for a boost over the rough spots he turned to pills. "Dexies," "uppers," "pep pills"—call them by any name, they spell trouble to the man who takes them to stay up too long too often.

Amphetamine abuse is only half the cycle. "Uppers" do the job too well. They speed the heartbeat, arouse the system, keep sleep and exhaustion beaten back for incredible periods of time. But when the time for relaxation finally comes, the person who got "up" chemically must get "down" the same way, and barbiturates are called upon to complete the cycle. The result is a constant, debilitating, emotional yo-yo, and some people never get off. "Speed freaks," the drug culture calls them, and to those who followed the country-music scene, the syndrome was sickeningly familiar.

Hank Williams, the greatest legend in country-western history, had been on pills long before his death by overdose at the age of twenty-nine. Other well-known musicians, like so many rock performers of a later era, had made pill-popping and heavy drinking staples of their daily routines. The crowds that flocked to the Cash concerts, the millions who bought the records, the truck drivers who bounced along the nation's highways to the sounds of the "Grand Ole Opry" every Saturday night—all knew the twisted, tragic road that pills could lead a man down. And so when Cash made that turn, the public seemed to look on with a resigned feeling that the inevitable would surely happen; and the sense of tragedy that was felt by the few who knew him well was numbed by a feeling that they had seen it all happen before.

By 1963 or '64 Cash was so dependent on pills that he began to carry a supply with him, no longer trusting their availability to chance when he needed them to keep going. His amphetamine use became less and less controlled, and it began to affect his career. He began to miss performances, and he was occasionally going on stage too hopped up to operate at the top of his ability. But audiences often confuse sweaty, frenetic motion for passion, and for awhile his performances when he was high seemed to go as well as when he was not.

The first arrest came in October of 1965. It was late at night, and Cash was crossing the United States–Mexico border at El Paso, Texas. He was coming from Juarez, Mexico, and stopped for a routine customs inspection. Stuffed into his guitar case in the back of his car (and in all his pockets, the folklore has it) were over one thousand pills—uppers and downers in almost equal amounts. He was arrested and jailed on the spot. He posted bail the next morning, and returned two months later to plead guilty to a charge of illegal possession of drugs. The penalty: a suspended thirty-day jail sentence and a fine of one thousand dollars.

The fine was the least of Cash's worries. The price he paid in bad publicity was much greater: Wire-service stories of the arrest and conviction went out all across America, and reporters badgered him with questions and popping flashbulbs as he left the courthouse after paying the fine. And suddenly all the world was reading about Cash's drug problem.

The experience sobered him. For a few months he steered clear of pills, but gradually his resolve dissipated, and he was on the downward spiral again.

There was another brush with the law soon afterward, this one in Starkville, Mississippi, following a concert at Mississippi State University. Picked up on the streets of the small town in the middle of the night, Cash was thrown in jail overnight, and fined and let go the next morning. The only charge ever made against him was for curfew violation, and Cash still feels that he was jailed wrongly. (He felt so strongly about it that night, in fact, that he broke his little toe and sprained an ankle beating a protest on the cell door with his feet.) The incident was a juicy one for the overactive rumor mill, and the image of Cash as a belligerent, drug-crazy maverick continued to grow.

The rigors of the road and the strain of show business began to rip at the already-weakened fabric of Cash's marriage. Vivian and his daughters (now there were four) saw less and less of him in their home in Casitas Springs, California. Cash had always been very close to his daughters, and for years the marriage with Vivian had survived largely because his love for them kept bringing him back to his California home. He finally left home, in June of 1966, and never came back. Vivian sued for divorce soon afterward, and Cash did not contest the suit. But it would be unfair and inaccurate to suppose that Cash experienced no agony over the marriage that didn't work. His sense of loyalty runs strong and deep, and the trauma of the empty marriage compounded his misery during the years when things were darkest.

By now Cash had graduated from one-at-a-time usage of amphetamines and was taking them by the handfuls, some days as many as ten an hour. He also began to show the side effects of his protracted dissipation—loss of appetite, chronic insomnia, loss of weight. He lost all interest in eating, going from over 200 pounds to less than 140. An automobile accident on a rain-slick Nashville street one night broke his nose and knocked out four teeth, and he almost died of an amphetamine overdose while struggling to recuperate from the injuries.

To a performer who is asking and receiving one-night guarantees in five figures, unreliability is the ultimate sin. Cash began by showing up for his shows late, or stoned, or both, staggering into the theater or auditorium barely coherent, just in time to perform. More than once his troupe would help him get dressed, point him in the direction of the stage, and watch while he knocked 'em dead, barely able to stand at the microphone, somehow still generating more musical excitement than anyone in the audience could remember ever feeling before.

Then came the no-shows—the dates when he just didn't arrive at all. No Cash usually meant no pay, and it is estimated that there were nearly forty such occasions in three years.

For the troupe traveling with him, it was a

nightmare that seemed never to end. The Cash road show was a large group now. It was an impressive team of musicians: Carl Perkins, a talented guitarist who left a lucrative solo career ("Blue Suede Shoes") to work as a sideman for Cash; the Tennessee Three, bigger than the original two with the addition of drummer "Fluke" Holland; the Statler Brothers, a quartet with a Grammy Award to its credit for "Flowers On The Wall," and the Carter Family, composed of the near-legendary Maybelle Carter and her daughters.

When Cash pulled his disappearing act (usually due to a mild amphetamine overdose that left him too zonked to perform), the job of explaining to an irate audience usually fell to these other troupers, and sometimes the loss in revenue for the team ran into tens of thousands of dollars. Often one of the members of the group would find Cash after a binge, haul him back onto the bus, and help him get dried out before time came to perform at the next stop. As the addiction grew worse, Cash's times off the road became long, unbroken amphetamine highs, and he had one close scrape with danger after another, living almost constantly on the pills. Tales began to circulate around Nashville (where he had bought a new house) about his being kicked out of nightclubs, put off airplanes, dragged home incoherent by friends.

It was after Cash was jailed a third time (this

one in Lafayette, Georgia, again an overnight stay) that he finally made a last effort to save himself from the total disaster that lay inevitably ahead. The story that follows is as old as redemption itself. It is so unbelievable, so like a fairy tale, that it is best told briefly and to the point: Johnny Cash kicked the amphetamine addiction, got off drugs and liquor to stay, and in so doing saw his faltering career resurrected right before his eyes.

The folklore of country music will always have it that June Carter brought him back to himself. Her role in Cash's comeback may be overplayed a bit, but it is true that, if any single person was the catalyst that touched off the healing process, it was June.

She had been a singer on the "Grand Ole Opry" and the Nashville-based circuit for years, and joined the Cash troupe in 1962 as a part of the Carter Family. She and Cash sang together on the road, becoming the top country duet in the business. From the first of Cash's troubles, June led a one-woman crusade to save him from his own worst inclinations. She begged and cajoled, then stormed and preached, and when none of that worked, tried flushing his pills down the toilet. Most of all she tried liberal applications of old-fashioned love. She loved the man. She fed him when he was too weak to eat, nursed him back to strength when he was sick, and eventually helped him find the will to turn things around.

Another important figure in the Cash reversal was Doctor Nat Winston, a Nashville psychiatrist who became Cash's friend, then tackled the job of pulling him through the withdrawal period. Nobody promised Cash it would be easy, and it wasn't. For two terrible weeks June, Maybelle, and other close friends stayed with him while Doctor Winston took him through the drying-out process. It was a ten-thousand-to-one shot, but some part of Cash responded to the crisis, and in two weeks he knew he was going to make it. His strength began to return. His emaciated frame slowly regained the robust look of earlier years. He stayed away from the pills three weeks, four weeks, two months, six months—until finally he knew that he was off for good. He had come all the way back. And now he faced the job of reconstructing his shambled career.

The Puritan ethic has it that virtue is its own reward. That is probably true, and by all the rules the restoration of his health should have been reward enough for Cash's successful struggle. But there was more, much more.

When Cash came back, he came all the way back—and then some. With his mind really clear for the first time in years, his troupe confident and happy, Cash zoomed almost immediately to the peak of his earlier form, and within months was bigger and better than he had ever been. His price for concerts climbed to $25,000 a show, five times what he had commanded during the bad ol' days. He and June won a Grammy for their version of "Jackson," and made the dream complete by getting married the same week. The Cash troupe went behind the bars of California's Folsom Prison to cut the first of two prison albums (the other was at San Quentin), and the result was a gold record almost before it had been marketed nationwide.

The cramped auditoriums of the Southeast gave way on Cash's concert schedule to such places as Carnegie Hall, Madison Square Garden, the London Palladium. The crowds were the same in all those places, and in Europe and Japan and Australia—big, warm and boisterously enchanted with the special Cash style. The records poured out of Columbia Studios, better now than ever, and the 1969 Country Music Association's award ceremony saw Cash winning best album (for the San Quentin LP; *Folsom* had won the same award the year before), best single (for "A Boy Named Sue"), male vocalist of the year, vocal group of the year (with June Carter), and entertainer of the year.

There was nothing left but TV and the movies, and that came too. The ABC television network needed a summer replacement to fill a gap left by the faltering "Hollywood Palace." Cash was tapped for the prime-time nationwide spot, and his show went on the air with such impact that it was renewed for the regular season, then renewed again for a third time around. The show was aired from the stage of the Opry House in Nashville, and provided unprecedented national coverage for the entire country-music community. Kirk Douglas came to town while the show was running, and persuaded Cash to star in a big-budget Western movie with him called *The Gunfight*.

Everywhere one looked, in every area of entertainment, Johnny Cash sat on top of the heap. And so it happened that it was in the middle of the most fantastic success story in show business history that God put His hand on Johnny Cash and let him know what it was to be a real disciple.

3

ON MAY 9, 1971, JOHNNY CASH SAT IN A PEW of a small Pentecostal church just outside Nashville. The preacher finished his sermon and began to make an altar call, appealing to the congregation to come down front and make things right with God.

Johnny Cash stood up, stepped into the aisle, and walked a few short steps to the wooden altar. He knelt heavily on the deep-red carpet and, in his own words, "made a complete dedication of my life to Jesus Christ."

For Cash it was both an end and a beginning. It was the end of a lifelong search for meaning, and the beginning of a discipleship that would come to dominate every part of his life. It was the beginning of the new Johnny Cash, the show biz superstar who would soon say about his new commitment: "I don't have a career anymore. What I have now is a ministry. Everything I have and everything I do is given completely to Jesus Christ now. I've lived all my life for the devil up 'til now, and from here on I'm going to live it for the Lord."

Those are strong and strange words indeed coming from the man whose public image was a jumble of legends that included violence and jail and drug addiction. Columbia Records once released a record entitled "Johnny Cash: Mean as Hell!" That is a pretty good tip-off to the myth which surrounded the man. He was not your freshly scrubbed All-American Boy, even with his recent success; and most people have thought him the most unlikely of all entertainers to make a move toward life-changing Christian faith. The truth is that Johnny Cash has never been the God-defying hellhound that many have assumed him to be. He is a sensitive, finely tuned man, and even in the worst days of his wanderings, he was more a miserable prodigal than a crusader for the evil life.

Cash's contact with old-time religion goes back to the earliest days he can remember as a boy on the farm in Dyess, Arkansas. His parents were decent, hardworking sharecroppers, and they gave him a bedrock attachment to basic values that

never left him. Music and religion were staples of
that early environment, and the two were inextri-
cably intertwined. Johnny's sister Joann Yates remembers those days well: "We belonged to the
Baptist church, and they really did some great
congregational singing. We used to hitch a ride to
church with our neighbors—sometimes to the
Baptist church and sometimes to a little Pentecostal church a little piece away on road #14.

"Sometimes we'd get scared to death in church.
The preacher preached hellfire and brimstone, and
that's the kind of religious services we grew up
with. We sang some of the same old songs that are
still around, like 'Amazing Grace' and 'Unclouded
Day.' Mama played the piano, mostly just chords,
but it was pretty good for back then." The songs of
the church were as much a part of the Cash family
as the cotton they chopped and the fierce loyalty
that was a family trademark.

"We bought a radio from Sears," Joann remembers, "and all of us used to sit in front of it
and eat popcorn and fudge and listen to shows like
'Inner Sanctum.'" She remembers less well the
flood of country music that poured into the Cash
home on that radio, but Johnny was soaking it all
up. "He entered every singing contest that came
along in school," she recalls. "He loved music and
always seemed to have a special gift for it, even
from the very first. He was so good that Mama

used to worry about him getting into music and leaving the Lord. And I guess you could say that's what happened. But nobody knows how many times she spent the night on her knees in prayer for him. In the days when things were going bad for him, all the press reports of the trouble he was in really hurt Mama. She read the papers and worried and prayed for him constantly."

Cash remembers that his religious ties as a youngster were real and meaningful, and he speaks of his recent spiritual experience as a "renewal." "I was first converted in that little Baptist church when I was about twelve or thirteen, and what I'm feeling as a Christian now is the same Spirit I felt back then."

There was one jolting, heart-crushing experience in those Dyess days that Cash almost never discusses, but which Joann considers to be an important part of his subsequent return to the Christian teachings of childhood. She tells the story: "Jack was John's next-oldest brother, and John nearly worshiped him. Jack was always very spiritual-minded, much more than the rest of us. I personally think he was called to preach, but I don't know that for sure.

"Jack was killed in an accident in 1944. He was just fourteen years old. John didn't get over it for years; he was terribly shook up—and I think he made a kind of silent promise to Jack when he was dying. The last thing Jack said to the family was 'Will you meet me in heaven?' We put those words on his tombstone. Now John has come back to God, and I think he's finally fulfilled a promise to Jack. Last night we were in the studio recording 'Amazing Grace' with the church choir. I looked over at him and he was closing his eyes to hide the tears while he sang along with us. I couldn't help but think then, 'The whole choir may be singing to God, but I believe John is singing to Jack.'"

It becomes clear that Johnny Cash's life-changing walk down the aisle that Sunday night was indeed a reawakening, and not a venture into entirely unknown territory. It was a response to a basic, gnawing hunger for God that, however deeply buried beneath his own personal rebellion, always flickered stubbornly somewhere inside him.

Most preachers avow that it does not matter why a man comes to God, that it is important only that he does. Theologically, that point can hardly be argued. But the time and circumstances of Cash's spiritual revival say much about the man and give what is perhaps a telling clue to the long-range seriousness of his commitment.

There is a scenario in the lore of Christianity that has been knocking around since Adam. It is a simple one: Man leaves God, seems to do well without Him, so disdains any tie with Him; then things go bad, trouble strikes, man finds himself in great need, so reaches out for God again. That plot is a legitimate one, and it has been played out by countless men in every age—the wayward soul in desperation turns to God. There can be no argument that Johnny Cash was a desperate man a few years ago. But he pulled himself (with the support from a few close friends) out of the disaster that he had created; he turned his fortunes dramatically around; and he soared to a level of professional success that would have left most men inebriated with a sense of well-being and personal satisfaction.

And it was then that he was irresistibly drawn to God—not when he was on bottom, but when he was on top. Men call on God because they are sick and need healing, when they are poor and need resources, when they are maligned and need comfort, when they are in a tailspin and need a personal reversal. Cash had come through those needs. And now he came to God because, when everything seemed right with his world again, he found that it was empty and without meaning. Some have tried to squeeze his story into the oldest of evangelistic clichés: On drugs he turned to God and lived religiously ever after. It just didn't happen that way. After the drugs, after the despair, after the dawning of the new day, Johnny Cash resisted the heady, "I showed 'em" attitude that one might expect in those circumstances. What Cash felt instead was gratitude, and a growing sense that he was put here on this earth for a purpose. And when he set out to find the meaning that his life lacked, he looked back to the faith that oozed around the corners of those old songs his mother used to sing, and he was on his way home again.

"After I had managed to overcome my pill habit and things started to go good again, I had to realize that it was the prayers of a lot of people that pulled me through. And so I felt like it must be for a purpose—that God had some purpose on earth for me. So when June and I got married we decided to do things differently. We had both been converted when we were younger, but we'd given our bodies to the devil, and we'd really been through hell. So we decided to try to go back—to try to feel that touch of God we'd felt so long before.

"We started going to lots of different churches in cities where we were on the road, and we went to lots of churches here in Hendersonville and Madison (suburbs of Nashville), looking for a place where we could be comfortable and, most of all, where we could really feel God."

That search for a place where they could feel God led Cash and his wife to Evangel Temple, a small Assembly of God congregation pastored by the Reverend Jimmy R. Snow, son of the great Hank Snow and himself a country singer. "The first time we went into that church we felt the Spirit of God. I don't know, maybe it scared us a little. The singing and the preaching and the praying were very emotional and you could just tell it ran deep and was sincere. But, you know, a lot of people get a little scared when they get around the Spirit like that, and maybe that's what happened to us. Anyway we didn't go back for a long time."

As the Cashes continued to look for a church that would help them back to God, events were unfolding that would soon bring them to Evangel Temple to stay. It was a young church, begun in 1965 by Snow, and occupied a small (only eight rows of pews, front to back) and unimpressive building on Dickerson Road in Hendersonville. Pastor Snow had a burden for the Nashville show-business community in which he had grown up, and God was moving on the tiny congregation to share that burden.

Snow went downtown often to the Grand Ole Opry House, both for the regular weekend "Opry" shows, and later for the Thursday taping sessions of Cash's television series. He was an old hand around the Opry, and quietly went about making friends for his little church and inviting his old show-business buddies to come to worship there. Cash remembers seeing him often, but Snow never pushed his religion at Cash, and never pressed him to attend Evangel Temple.

Among those whom Snow did urge to come to church were Larry and Dottie Lee, old Opry friends who were playing in the backup band for singer Charlie Louvin at the time. Dottie recalls, "When Jimmy used to come around, we wanted to hide. . . . We knew God was dealing with us, and we just didn't want to be reminded. But we needed help badly in our lives, and we finally reached a point of desperation and decided to go to church. We really found something there, and so we became regular members."

Soon afterward, Johnny Cash's guitarist and closest friend, Luther Perkins, was killed when a fire swept his Nashville home. The sudden tragedy stunned Cash. "We had pretty much lost touch with John," Dottie says, "but we were very close to Luther, and when he died it took us out to Johnny and June's house three or four nights in a row, and we got real close. Strange as it sounds, that opened the door eventually for us to witness to them. Larry went to work at House of Cash (Johnny's multicorporate business complex), and we all became close friends again."

At about this time God was also working on Joann Yates, Cash's younger sister who lived in Nashville and worked at House of Cash. "I was always the black sheep of the family," she says, "and at this particular time I was really at a crossroad in my personal life. I was ready to make a break in one direction or another." On a trip to Arkansas in a small, private plane, Joann got a bad scare. The plane hit a thunderstorm and was barely able to handle the turbulence. For a few minutes it looked to Joann like it was to be her last plane ride, and while the wind threw the little plane around she promised God that she was going to straighten her life out.

Enter Dottie Lee. She sensed that Joann was ready to hear the gospel, and soon after that traumatic plane ride had Joann visiting Evangel Temple. Joann remembers that first visit well, and what she remembers best of all is the same feeling that her brother would have later—an awe, almost a fear, at being in the presence of the Spirit of God. Halfway through the service she excused herself to powder her nose, slipped out the back door, and headed for home.

But Dottie persisted, and Joann went back a second time, and a third, and God dealt powerfully with her to make a full commitment to Him. A few weeks later she did, and she has been a mainstay of the congregation ever since. She sings in the alto section of the church choir, works in all phases of its evangelistic outreach, and her husband Harry became the director of its youth program. When she made a change, she made a 180-degree turnaround, and she is as passionately attached to Evangel Temple and its ministries now as she was oblivious to it in earlier days.

Joann's thrill at her new way of life was irrepressible, and she virtually shouted her enthusiasm to any family member who would listen. Her niece (and Johnny's daughter) Rosie went to church with her several times and liked it. Rosie began to urge her parents to return to Evangel Temple, and they finally decided to go and find out for themselves what special fascination the place held for Rosie.

Rosie wasn't the only child in the Cash household who helped prod Johnny and June toward a dedication to God. There was a very tiny Cash who had come to the marriage almost as a special gift. He weighed in at 7 pounds, 10 ounces on March 3, 1970, at 12:43 P.M. in the Madison Hospital. From the day he was born, that son was pride, joy, life itself to Johnny, and with the baby's arrival, the place of God in his home seemed even more urgently important than before. "I guess when that little boy out at our house came along," he would tell a reporter later, "we realized we weren't teen-agers anymore. It was like it almost always is, the grown-ups get shown the way by the children." When Johnny and June left the hospital with their tiny bundle, their last stop was the hospital chapel, where the two of them went in, knelt, and quietly, in their own way, dedicated little John Carter Cash to Jesus Christ.

And so Johnny Cash finally began to attend Evangel Temple regularly early in 1971, and the singing of the believers and the preaching of Pastor Snow and the urging, probing presence of the Holy Spirit moved him closer and closer to God.

After he and Snow became close friends, one day Cash called the pastor and asked him to come out to his house, a massive, rugged structure built on a ledge overlooking Old Hickory Lake, with woods all around it. Deep in those woods was an old shack, and there it was that Cash spent hours on end, searching himself, seeking God, thrashing through the thicket of doubts, and weaknesses that must be penetrated if a man such as Cash is to surrender completely to God. "This is my private place of prayer," he told Snow, and explained to him the decision he had come to over the past year—a decision to follow Jesus Christ closely and allow Him to do things through his life. "He asked me to dedicate that shack to the Lord," Snow related, "and we knelt right out there and prayed together. When we did, God's Spirit met with us, and confirmed the experience we had there. I could really feel God."

It is an article of faith in the fundamentalist churches that public testimony of regeneration is a powerful and important dynamic in the process of one's dedication to God. And so Snow, fully believing that Cash's experience with God was to be a permanent and strong one, urged him to make a public dedication. "There was no doubt in my mind that he was really turning his whole life over to the service of God," Snow says "and I told him what a wonderful thing it would be for him to make the act of commitment in God's house."

And so it was that, on a Sunday night in May of 1971, Johnny Cash made the move down the aisle at Evangel Temple. Pastor Snow recalls that he had preached a sermon on the Christian home and was giving an altar call, as he always does, at the end of the message. When Cash moved into the aisle and to the altar, Snow met him there. He was told, "I want to live my life right, and the first thing I've got to do is be a spiritual leader in my own home." June slipped from her seat and joined her husband, and they knelt there between the pastor and the churchful of worshipers and sealed their rededication to God.

Later Pastor Snow was quoted as saying, "It is one thing for a public figure to join a church; it is another thing for him to humble himself enough to get down on his knees and crawl and cry in front of a congregation."

Amen!

4

WHEN JOHNNY CASH LEFT THE LITTLE brick building that night, the Evangel Temple Assembly of God was his church, and the Reverend Mr. Jimmy R. Snow was his pastor. Both the shepherd and the flock deserve a closer look.

Jimmy Snow is thirty-six years old, with blue grey eyes that are never still and sandy brown hair that is already thinning on top. He is a flesh-and-blood perpetual-motion machine, as energetic and tireless as any man who ever wore the cloth. He has dreams, big dreams, and they are all for his church, Evangel Temple, his life's work and the object of his relentless obsession. Snow gives the impression that there is only one thing that he cares about, one thing worth pursuing, and that is the work of his congregation.

It was not always thus. As the son of Hank Snow, he was born with the glare of the spotlight and the whine of the electric guitar already in his blood. The uncommon intensity and drive that Jimmy Snow exhibits now he had even as a teenager, and he seemed destined from childhood for a career onstage. The Grand Ole Opry was a second home to him. It whetted his ambition (and fortunately his musical skills as well), and by his middle teens Jimmy Snow felt like he was ready to take Nashville music by the tail.

He started out in promising fashion. Working in small towns, rodeos, circuses, all the stops so familiar to a rookie country singer in the mid-1950s, Snow began to build a reputation of his own. He came back to Nashville for guest shots at the Opry, and traveled for three years as a preliminary act for Elvis Presley (who was still undiscovered as a national rock idol) and other big-name performers. Cash remembers Snow well from these days and their paths occasionally crossed but they never became close friends. Snow signed a seven-year contract with RCA recording studios, made an appearance on the nationwide "Lawrence Welk Show," and appeared to be on his way to the big time.

That was the story of his public career. His pri-

JOHNNY CASH with BILLY GRAHAM at Explo '72. The Jesus Music Festival attracted almost 200,000 people. *(Campus Crusade Photo)*

CASH, his wife JUNE CARTER, and son JOHN, JR., arrive at the preview of their film, *The Gospel Road*—"The most important thing in our lives right now." *(Photo by Dale Ernsberger, The Tennessean)*

The man in black comes on stage at the Grand Ole Opry, a converted gospel tabernacle which is the center of Nashville's music scene. *(Photo by Les Leverett)*

It's always the same—the people reach out to him with their hands and their spirits, and he reaches back in quick, hard handclasps. *(Photo by Les Leverett)*

JOHNNY CASH's pastor, BROTHER JIMMY SNOW, gives altar call during his radio show "Grand Ole Gospel Time," broadcast from the Grand Ole Opry House. CASH looks on as many people in the audience respond to the invitation. *(Photo by Les Leverett)*

The Evangel Temple choir appears on stage with JOHNNY CASH. The members of the group will put just as much effort into their singing the following day, when they perform for elderly patients at Bordeaux Metro Hospital. *(Photo by Les Leverett)*

CASH's theatrical presence has a great deal to do with his popularity. He has the assurance of a man who has more than fame—he has the Spirit of God within him. *(Photo by Les Leverett)*

There's nothing the surging crowd loves more than to see JOHNNY CASH and JUNE CARTER perform together. JUNE joined her husband at the altar the night he rededicated his life to the Lord. *(Photo by Les Leverett)*

A reflective moment before JOHNNY and BILLY GRAHAM go out to talk to the people, each in his own way—JOHNNY through his music, and BILLY as one of the most powerful preachers of our day.

Maybe BILLY is thinking of his own grandchildren as he admires young JOHN CARTER CASH with his Daddy.

It's been a long day and BILLY GRAHAM and JOHNNY CASH are ready for a good dinner.

No one who was there will ever forget Explo '72. One of the highlights was the joint appearance of singing star JOHNNY CASH and Evangelist BILLY GRAHAM.

The Gospel Road

A 20th Century-Fox Film Corporation Production

Johnny during the filming of *The Gospel Road*

Mr. and Mrs. Johnny Cash

Robert Elfstrom as Jesus Christ

June Carter Cash as Mary Magdalene

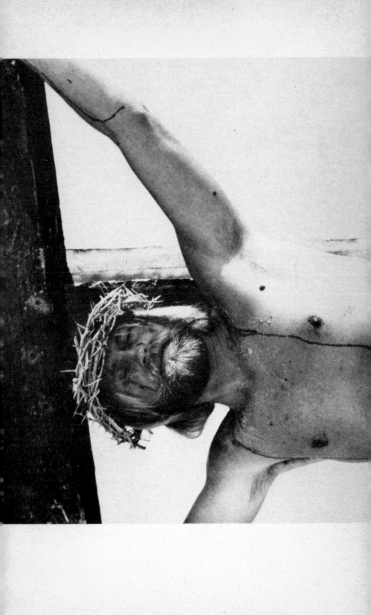

vate life was something else again. It was that sad old story: liquor, pills, and burning the candle at both ends had already begun to tell on the twenty-three-year-old singer. "I got to where I was either singing or drunk all the time," he says. "It was one or the other. I got on pep pills, got a bad habit, and couldn't seem to break it." (The problem was not a new one for Snow. "I had been kicked out of Goodlettsville High School when I was a teen-ager, and almost got kicked out of Litton High. They just let me quit without putting it on my official record. I was just a cheap drunk, lying and cheating and having trouble all the time.")

From his normal weight of 150 pounds, Snow went down to 117 pounds, and finally came to a bone-jarring confrontation with himself that ended in an abortive suicide attempt. It was then that, "kneeling out in a friend's yard by the mailbox in the middle of the night," Jimmy Snow accepted Jesus Christ as his Saviour. That decision was a private affair between him and God. He married Carol Leigh Cooper, the daughter of a popular "Grand Ole Opry" singing team, and continued to pursue his career. But as his discipleship grew, he became more and more involved in the activities of the church, and when, less than six months later, he announced that he was leaving show business to enter the ministry, the story made page one of the *Tennessean,* Nashville's statewide daily newspaper. It was datelined September 23, 1958:

James Rogers (Jimmy) Snow, twenty-three, guitar-playing son of Hank Snow, said last night that he will become an Assembly of God minister. Snow, who has been singing in shows ever since he was three years old, said, "The Lord called me to preach." The youth said the call came September 1 in answer to a prayer a week earlier. He said that he first thought of entering the ministry when he was asked two months ago to speak to a youth group at First Assembly of God Church in Madison. "I was used to singing for stage shows and was not a speaker," said Snow. "I don't believe I could make more than a five-minute talk on religion, but I spoke thirty-five minutes to that group.

"I decided that if I could talk that long on religion, I must really be interested in it, and after reading the Bible more I really studied it for the first time.

"Then in a prayer I said to God that if I got another preaching engagement by September 1, I'd consider myself called to be a minister.

"Then on September 1 a member of the First Assembly of Madison asked me to preach a revival in a trailer court. In fact I preached there twice."

Jimmy preached his fourth sermon on Sunday at another Assembly of God church, the Westside Assembly.

"I hope to go to Central Bible Institute of the

Assemblies of God in Springfield, Missouri, in September," Jimmy said.

He is a noted performer in his own right and has been doing most of his professional singing the last seven years. One of his records for Victory is a song he wrote, "The Rules of Love."

Snow immediately hit the road as an evangelist, preaching in over a hundred Assembly of God churches during the next eight years. He confesses that at first he relied heavily on his singing and show business image to bring people out to hear him. "I remember one night after the service I was in the bathroom, and I overheard two guys talking, and one said, 'Just like I thought—that Snow fellow is about 80 percent sing and about 20 percent preach.' That was a real put-down, but I knew it was true, and I knew I had to learn to get into the Word." In those early days of his ministry he knew little about the Bible and less about preaching, and thus developed out of necessity a penchant for Bible study that still characterizes his ministry today.

In January of 1965, while Johnny Cash was still on his downhill trip, Snow, by then a polished evangelist, was conducting a crusade in Oklahoma City. There the Lord burdened his heart with the need for a church in Nashville that could minister especially to the music community. (The impulse was not a new one. When he left Music City to evangelize eight years earlier, he had felt that someday he would be back as a pastor.) That sense of mission would not leave him, and he finished the meeting, abruptly canceled his scheduled revival dates, and left for Nashville to do the job.

When he arrived, Snow had lots of faith and guts and very little of anything else. He picked up a ninety-day option to buy a vacant lot, where he put up an old revival tent and began to preach. Good crowds came out to hear him, and many were saved and baptized with the Holy Spirit. With thirty days left on the option (he was by then convinced that the lot should be the site of the new building), Snow organized his church with six members. That number went up to twenty-three with a week left to buy the property, but still no money in the till. In that last week an anonymous donor gave the infant church a gift of $39,000, and Snow praised the Lord all the way to the real estate office, where he secured the purchase of the property on which his church now stands. Only a few miles away, Johnny Cash was struggling to free himself from pills and despair.

Snow floated a $75,000 loan and got the building underway. "We had nothing but hard times at first," he reminisces with a smile. "We got the basement finished when the recession hit and we ran out of money and had to quit building. We sat in that basement for a year and a half with nothing but a concrete-block shell overhead." In September of 1967 the structure was finally completed, a pentagonal sanctuary with dark-red bricks outside and a high, exposed-beam ceiling within. The building stands on a busy four-lane highway, flanked by a mobile home sales lot on one side and a new Chevron station on the other.

In 1970, while Johnny Cash was reaching the peak of his career with successful TV show and concert dates, the church was growing slowly, and by the end of 1970 claimed barely one hundred members. "January of '71—that's when things really began to move," Snow reflects. "Some of the folks had been burdened for revival; it seemed like we had just stopped growing. The Lord spoke to us one night and said that within six months our church would become a lighthouse to the city of Nashville, and would eventually be known all over the United States. Man, that sounded impossible then, but it lit a fire under all of us and we started praying and fasting—pretty soon a revival came and it hasn't stopped since.

"During that year, 1971, people from the entertainment industry began to get saved, and they'd pass the word about what they had found at Evangel Temple. The faster we grew, the more we prayed. Things just broke loose. We've had almost

constant revival since then, and there's hardly anyone in Nashville who doesn't know about us."

He is right. In a city that has more than its share
of big, beautiful churches (both the Southern
Baptist and the Church of Christ denominations
are headquartered in Nashville), the impact of
Snow's small fundamentalist group is incredibly
great. Sunday-school attendance has quadrupled
since 1971, the sanctuary has been expanded to
twice its original size, and the ministries of the
church have multiplied.

The heart of any church is its worship, and wor-
shiping at Evangel Temple is an unforgettable experience. If the pastor were any less a preacher
than Snow is, music would dominate the worship,
because it is a church chock-full of Nashvillians
who are musicians first, last, and always. Besides
the Cash family, other big names worship there:
Peggy Little and Connie Smith are stalwarts
(when Connie was married last fall, Rex Humbard
flew down to assist Snow with the ceremony), and
Skeeter Davis, Kris Kristofferson, and many more
come from time to time. Apart from these, there
are dozens of others who are employed in the recording industry—technicians, backup instrumen-
talists, musicians who work the recording sessions.
Old-fashioned, hand-clapping, heartfelt, camp-

meeting singing comes to the congregation as naturally as breathing itself; and the music in the sanctuary on any Sunday morning or night is an exciting, pulsating reminder that old-time religion is alive and well in Music City.

Naturally there is a choir. Not just one of those two-anthems-and-a-Latin-liturgy choirs that decorate churches these days, but a hard-driving, gung-ho crew that sings like there is no tomorrow. Their music virtually throbs with a unique mixture of enthusiasm, volume, and electric accompaniment in equal parts. The choir has a devoted constituency (three meetings per week) that includes longhairs and middle-aged men, teen-age girls and grandmothers—singers of every description. The sound which Snow pulls from the group (he directs it himself) is dominated by female voices, especially the warm, rich tones that pour from the altos on every tune.

Johnny Cash is a kind of patron saint to the Evangel Temple choir. The choir has appeared with him on stage, and in 1972 provided a choral background for his recording of "A Thing Called Love," a Columbia release. The tune climbed to number one on the *Billboard* country-music charts, and later in the year was the title tune for a Cash album. The choir has taped other songs at the House of Cash recording studio, and hopes to release its own album of gospel favorites soon.

When the congregation has sung (sometimes six or seven songs, with a few gospel choruses thrown in for good measure), and the choir has finished, Brother Snow goes to work. And work he does, preaching with the headlong, pile-driving style of an evangelist. His sermons are always closely Bible-based; he will sometimes take a thirty-verse passage and expound on each verse separately, right down the line. He gestures fiercely and paces across the platform, back and forth, now shouting, now whispering, always holding his congregation in full control. He begins to perspire and off comes the jacket, out comes the handkerchief, and the flow of words and passion never abates for a moment. All of this takes time (he sometimes preaches for an hour and a half), but when he is finished the people know they have heard a message—not just a sermon—but a message.

After the preaching there is an altar call. And after the altar call there are almost always seekers to pray with, for it is difficult to worship at Evangel Temple and not be moved.

The most glamorous aspect of the Evangel Temple program is its radio show. Pastor Snow and the choir do a thirty-minute live broadcast from the stage of the Grand Ole Opry every Friday night that is beamed to millions of listeners. The arrangement is perfect: When the Friday night "Grand Ole Opry" performance ends at ele-

ven o'clock, the crowd stays to hear Snow, his
choir, and a different show biz guest each week.
They get a live audience for their radio program,
and the audience gets an additional thirty minutes
of music and preaching.

That such a show could ever be arranged with
the Opry and the radio station is a miracle in itself.
Snow first took the idea to Cash, and he agreed to
help set it up if he could. The two of them fasted
and prayed about it, decided it was worth a try,
and went to see the manager of the Opry, Bud
Wendell. "The Lord moved in his heart, and he
gave us the go-ahead," Snow recalls. It was that
simple. The key to the show's success, and to stay-
ing on the air, was getting country-western stars to
appear. Cash himself set the example, doing the
kick-off show on February 11, 1972. That started
the ball rolling, and by now almost every Nashville star has donated his services to "Grand Ole
Gospel Time," as the broadcast is called. (To
name a few: Webb Pierce, Buck Owens, Kris Kristofferson, Pat Boone, Charley Pride.)

What the Opry audience (and the people at
home) hear is not just music. If the guest has a
Christian testimony, he gives it during the show,
and after twenty-or-so minutes of singing, Snow
preaches and in that unlikely setting gives an altar
invitation. The formula works. Hundreds have
made confessions of faith in the Friday-night ser-

vices, sometimes praying in their seats, sometimes walking the aisles to pray at the apron of the stage. Evangel Temple church members fan out into the audience during the sermon to act as personal workers when the invitation is given. (150 of Snow's congregation studied a course on altar work and personal witnessing which he taught to prepare them for this work.)

Opry officials are as pleased with the unique venture as Snow is. In its first two months the show drew mail from as far away as California, from over half of all the fifty states, at the rate of thirty letters per week. Since then the show has been picked up by a powerful station in Portugal, and is now taped, translated, and beamed to Europe in a delayed broadcast every week. According to Opry manager Wendell, mail response has grown steadily (it now runs to eighty letters per week), and the show is becoming a feature that visitors to the Opry expect and look forward to.

The "new" has worn off the show now, and for the regulars, it is hard, time-consuming work that occupies every Friday night. But still they come, all of them, every week, to pray and rehearse and sing and pray again. Why? Larry Lee, who coordinates the guest appearances, speaks for all of them when he answers the question: "It's my calling, you might say. At some point in his life a man

wants to contribute something. I can't preach, I
can't sing; so I organize and coordinate. It needs to
be done and I can do it. It's that simple." It was
Larry who found an opportunity to witness to
Johnny and June.

The "Grand Ole Gospel Time" broadcast is a
spectacular, out-front ministry of Evangel Temple.
And perhaps this is the kind of ministry that the
church performs best, steeped as it is in the tradition of show business and musical performance.
But the floodlit stage is by no means the only place
where Cash's church does the work of the kingdom. Perhaps it is away from the glitter and glamour of the Opry House that the true personality of
the congregation is best understood. To illustrate:

*It is a winter Saturday in Nashville, but the sun
shines pleasantly and the wind that blows is warm
and springlike. It is early afternoon and a few cars
are scattered over the asphalt parking lot at the
red-brick church building.*

*Inside a group of twenty-three men and women
sit around the Reverend Mr. Snow as he talks.
They are all dressed casually; all carry Bibles, and
now they are praying together, each one quietly
mouthing his own supplication. "Okay, folks, let's
go," Snow says at the "Amen," and they move out*

onto the sun-drenched parking lot and into five automobiles and away.

Destination: Bordeaux Metro Hospital, an enormous convalescent hospital in Nashville, most of whose five hundred patients are old and uncared for. Depression is the dominant mood at Bordeaux, despite the cheerfulness of the staff, because most who walk in as patients are ultimately carried out as corpses, and that grim reality is difficult to ignore in the faces of those who were once young and strong and healthy but are no more. The Evangel Temple group is going to Bordeaux to tell the people there that God loves them and that they, God's children, love them as well. It is a simple message, but it is one which at Bordeaux is lacking and needed and oh, so welcome!

Nurses greet the visitors warmly as they enter; they have come here often and are well remembered. There are many wards at Bordeaux, and the Evangel Temple group goes to the first one and begins. Plugging a portable cassette player into a wall socket, one of the girls flops a tape onto the machine and signals that it is rolling. For the next six minutes the ward rings with the best sounds that Music Row can afford, as the choir sings to a custom-made tape accompaniment. They sing the songs that they have learned to love back in the Evangel Temple worship services, singing as lustily as on any stage or studio. The listeners are in beds, in braces, in wheelchairs—and many of them are in tears.

When the music stops, the choir members spread out into the ward, talking, listening, praying with patients. There is no sermon, no harangue, no mention of denomination or creed—just lots of hand-squeezing, neck-hugging, reading of the Bibles they carry, and "I love you" whispered over and over. It is a beautiful scene. A nurse looking on shakes her head and observes, "Lots of these people stay in here for years and never have a visitor. Most of them are just waiting to die. I'll tell you, they really look forward to Brother Snow's people coming around. It's a great thing they do."

Twenty minutes later the group moves on to the next ward to repeat the scene, as they will over and over, all through the afternoon, until the hospital's dinner hour forces them to leave.

As they drive back to the church and then home, darkness is already crowding out the short winter day. What they have done this day would not be called fun. Certainly it is not glamourous. It is draining, hard work, and their energy and emotions are spent. Next Saturday they will be at the Spencer Youth Home on a similar mission—and the next Saturday, back at Bordeaux again.

Many of those in the two-thousand-plus audience at the Opry the night before might be surprised to know that the Evangel Temple choir places such a premium on Christian witness of this type. Those who know the members best will agree that it fits perfectly the spirit and the style of discipleship that has made the church grow. They sing about a thing called love, and they believe totally in what it can do.

5

WHEN A SUPERSTAR LIKE JOHNNY CASH
dedicates himself to personal Christian discipleship, problems arise that the average convert
never encounters.

The first thing Cash did when he joined Evangel
Temple was tell his pastor that he wanted to pull
his share of the load as a member. "I'm part of you
now," he told Snow, "and I want to do my share.
Just use me and abuse me—anything I can do for
the Lord, I want to do it." That extended to financial support, he explained. He wanted to pay
tithes to the church "just like you expect everyone
else to do."

Snow laughs now when he remembers it,

though he was admittedly pleased (and perhaps a bit tempted) by the offer. "I told him that was out of the question," Snow says. "I said, 'Man, you'll wreck my whole church if you do that. If the word gets out that you're paying tithes here, people will think we've got it made. Nobody else will ever give another dime.'" And so the pastor convinced his new member that tithing wouldn't be a good idea and persuaded him to channel his religious giving into other areas. (At an income that reportedly has gone as high as $3 million annually, a 10 percent tithe would represent an amount three times the total Evangel Temple budget.) Cash now gives anonymous support to a variety of religious charities and projects.

Money is not the only source of Cash's problems in becoming an average Joe in the church pew. The simple act of worship itself becomes a potential problem when people come to Evangel Temple to see him rather than to take part in the service. The word spread quickly around Nashville, and a sign now adorns the church lobby: ABSOLUTELY NO AUTOGRAPHS OR PICTURES TAKEN INSIDE THE SANCTUARY. For the most part, Snow says, that keeps the curious from approaching Johnny and June, and the church members themselves have never been a problem.

"It's probably the only church in the world where John can come and worship and not be bothered by people," his sister Joann says. He agrees.

"I can pretty much be myself at Evangel Temple. I'm just 'old home folks' to the people there, and they don't pay much attention to me. Oh, every now and then somebody will come up to me at church and try to pitch a song to me or something like that. One time a fella walked up before service and pushed a tape into my hand." He grins crookedly at the memory. "Said he was a songwriter and wanted me to listen to his stuff. I grabbed him by the arm, marched him right down front and sat him on the bench. He had to listen to the whole sermon right there. I think the Lord did something for him that day, you know. I think he got something he didn't come looking for!"

When it comes to the conduct of his personal life, Cash has shown that he can be as straight now as he was wild in earlier days. His language, once salted with four-letter expletives, now is conspicuously free of profanity. He no longer smokes or drinks alcohol of any kind, and declines to serve drinks in his home or offices. The office complex at House of Cash includes a recording studio, and musicians often like a little pick-me-up to help sessions along the way, but Cash still refuses to allow liquor on the premises. "That's just the way he feels about it," a colleague says, "and anyone who can't buy that can just record somewhere else."

Cash makes it clear that his change of life-style is a permanent one: "I guess I've committed every sin there is to commit, and I know what it's like on the other side of the street. I know what's good for a man and what's bad for a man. I know what will break up a marriage. I know what will ruin a home. I know what will tear up a man's life. And I'm not going to have any of that stuff around anymore."

How have Cash's own sidemen and professional associates reacted to the new life-style? "Well, just fine," he responds. "Nobody around here has made any objections at all to the way we're doing now. Some of them are what you might call lukewarm Christians, but they're all very sympathetic to what I'm doing. They know that it's a part of me, and they respect that. As a matter of fact, most of them like it better now. We've found out around here that Jesus Christ is good for people."

Both Johnny and June emphatically avow that Pastor Snow's preaching is the best anywhere, and that he could be a nationally known pulpiteer if he sought greater exposure. Their respect for the hard-working pastor is obvious. "I'd like to produce a gospel-music special for TV sometime," Cash says, "and have Jimmy preach at the end of the show. More people need to hear the Word—just songs by themselves won't do the job."

When John Doe has a religious experience, the

last thing he worries about is the danger of his experience being misinterpreted in Dubuque and Timbuktu. But Johnny Cash never gets too far from the public eye. His name, as they say, is a household word. As his involvement in his new faith grows, another problem that Cash has had to deal with is that of being misunderstood by his public.

Entertainers who claim religious experiences often find their experiences stretched out of proportion by a sensation-hungry press. The star is misquoted and misrepresented; and the public is misled and consequently disappointed to discover that the "conversion" was not all that the reports implied. The result is bad publicity for everybody concerned.

Nashville had one such jolting case in 1970, when country-rock star Jerry Lee Lewis was reported to have been converted (also in the Assembly of God) and given up show business forever. Lewis confirmed the report, and rashly announced that he was turning to clean living and the pulpit. That premature claim, in the words of one Nashville observer, "sent shock waves throughout the music world and was the cause of endless speculation." His "new life" disintegrated within two months. To the puzzled questions of those who had taken him at his word, he could only explain: "Yeah, I'm back to smoking, drinking, playing in clubs, and running around with women. I meant it when I said it, and I was going good there for awhile, but I just couldn't keep it up. I tried and failed. At least I'm man enough to admit it."

Cash has always considered his religious life a totally personal affair, and has consequently been disinclined to discuss it freely or glibly with reporters. The charge that is sometimes leveled at minor-league entertainers—that they "get religion" for the publicity that might revive a sagging career—can certainly never be laid to Cash. He has sought not to publicize his experience, and declined to court even the rich exposure of a *Time* magazine cover article when that publication tried to nail his story down.

At the same time, Cash is deeply and permanently immersed in his discipleship, and gradually the news of it has seeped out. His appearance at Explo '72 in Dallas was nationally televised, and in the past year he has made public statements about his faith that have sent out unmistakable signals about what has happened to him.

Does Cash feel that his career is damaged in any way by his religious experience? "Not one bit. I'm not giving up any aspect of my career. As far as losing my following or something like that—well, that doesn't worry me at all." What about his image as a "tough guy"? Does he feel that it is threatened by his new life-style? "Well, if what you're talking about is being a man, becoming a Christian doesn't make me one bit less a man than I've ever been. Being a Christian isn't for sissies. It takes a real man to live for God—a lot more man than to live for the devil, you know? If you really want to live right these days, you gotta be tough. And as far as that image of me as some kind of mean guy always going around fighting and tearing things up—well, that's been exaggerated anyway."

So the career and the ministry will go on together. And there is no better example of the effective —and dramatic—way in which a man of Cash's clout can combine the two than his recent visit to Las Vegas.

Even in his most abandoned days, Cash had no taste for Las Vegas. Perhaps the scruples drilled into him as an Arkansas boy made a greater impact than even he imagined—for whatever cause, he had steadfastly refused to perform in the city he calls "Sodom and Gomorrah." But that attitude changed unexpectedly. "After I got acquainted with the Lord, I began to realize that, now that I have something to give those people, Las Vegas is exactly where I should go. So I agreed to play the Hilton International showroom the week of Easter and, while I was entertaining, tell the people something about Jesus."

As the time for the Las Vegas date approached,

Cash became increasingly impressed with the importance of what he was about to do. Pastor Snow flew out for the opening to lend moral support. When opening night came, the house (the biggest showroom in Vegas) was packed out, and Cash came on to do his regular program. His approach was different from the Las Vegas formula which is almost never violated—he had no comic act to precede him, no orchestra to accompany his group, none of the fancy clothes which are trademarks of Vegas performers. And when he came to the final five minutes of each show, things *really* got different. He sang brief excerpts from Christian songs while pictures of Jesus were projected onto the wall behind him, and quietly told the audience of his love for the Lord.

The response from the audience that first night was warm and positive, and so it went through the week. Standing-room-only crowds filled the showplace three times a night, and each time left sobered and provoked—some to anger but most to serious thought. The hotel management, skeptical at first, warmed to what Cash was doing, and bought a full-page ad in the Nashville *Tennessean* a week later to urge him publicly to accept a return engagement. Reviews of the Cash performance were almost gushingly favorable. Typical was that of the prestigious Los Angeles *Times*, which called it "a triumph of the highest order" and praised Cash as a man of "deep integrity and purpose ... unwilling to compromise with the Las Vegas showroom tradition. . . . Rarely have we seen an opening with as much emotional impact," the lengthy review concluded.

Cash looks back on the incident as an example of how his career can be used for Christian witness. "It was something I wanted to do, that's all. I got some compliments and some criticism, but I know what I'm doing, and I know that God is with me. I'd give my testimony in the filthiest club in the country—as a matter of fact, I'd enjoy the opportunity. If I keep on, I know the devil's going to get mad, and I'm ready for it. I expect someone to throw something at me or take a shot at me in a situation like that one of these days.

"But my testimony doesn't offend people, because I tell it in love and I don't put people down with it. I'm not dogmatic when I testify. I just tell people how I feel and leave it with them. I know where I am when I go into a place of sin like that, and it's not inappropriate the way I do it. I just make it a part of my concert and then tell them 'This is what I love most.' I think Jesus would do something like that. He had more love for the sinner than He did for the hypocrite."

The Las Vegas performance was one of Cash's first occasions of public testimony, and its dramatic setting caused it to be reported—and, as it turned out, misreported—in the religious press. That misinformation led to a telephone interview with a Nashville reporter who himself misquoted Cash, sending a report all over the nation that he had denied receiving the Holy Spirit.

It should be pointed out that Evangel Temple is a Pentecostal church, and the practice of speaking in unknown tongues as one is baptized with the Holy Spirit is central to its doctrine and worship. After his rededication in mid-1971, Cash and his wife both began a serious, intense study of the Bible, and experienced what Pastor Snow calls "an enormous amount of spiritual growth." During this time they began to seek the Holy Spirit baptism—as Cash said in a religious magazine, "If the time to receive the Holy Ghost can be pushed and promoted, then we did that—we courted the idea."

In the fall of 1971, Snow received a call from Cash asking the pastor to meet him at the church and pray for him to receive this experience. The two met with a group of Evangel Temple men, and there he was baptized with the Holy Spirit. Since that time Cash has described this infilling of the Spirit as a growing, vital source of strength and direction. It was a significant step for Cash, and he made it without looking back.

By the time this news made its way to a charismatic convention in Minneapolis, however, it had been hopelessly confused. Cash was asked about the garbled reports of his Holy Spirit baptism, and tried gamely to straighten them out. He picked up the Nashville *Tennessean* one morning in August 1972, and saw a headline staring back at him: CASH DENIES BAPTISM, ALTAR CALL. He read the story that followed:

> Singer Johnny Cash denied reports yesterday that he had received the "baptism of the Holy Spirit" or given an "altar call" in Las Vegas. Cash's reply came in the wake of a Religious News Service story from Minneapolis . . . that Cash, appearing in Las Vegas, received "a wave of the Spirit" after he had sung several gospel songs. The article (said) that Cash gave "an altar call" and that some 1500 persons received Jesus. Yesterday in Nashville Cash said, "We always close our concert with gospel songs, and the response to them is a spirit of emotion." The singer said he underwent no charismatic experience and, as for the altar call: "We sang our final, 'A Thing Called Love,' and at the end of it I was shaking hands with a number of people who congratulated us."

This was precisely the kind of distortion that Cash so feared. He barely finished reading the story before he swung into action. Joann Yates, working as the receptionist for House of Cash at the time, remembers the morning well. "John came bursting through the door and almost shouted, 'Joann, I didn't say it.' I hadn't seen the paper and didn't know what he was talking about. 'Didn't say what?' I asked him—and he showed the article to me. He stomped around here trying to keep his temper and wrote a letter to the paper —he wanted to get the words just right. He was really upset."

His statement appeared in full in the next-day's paper:

> I feel that part of my statement over the telephone yesterday was misunderstood, and I would like to set the record clear.
>
> The headline stating "Johnny Cash Denies Baptism" is pretty strong language. I was asked if I had received the baptism of the Holy Spirit on stage at Las Vegas, and if I gave an altar call. The answer was "no"—but I didn't mean that the Holy Spirit wasn't alive in me and guiding me.
>
> Months before that, in Jimmy Snow's church, I had received the baptism of the Holy Spirit, and that was the most beautiful feeling I have ever known in my life—to feel that the Spirit of God had come to live in me.
>
> Several months following that I felt a strong indwelling of the Holy Spirit, like the time last November when I was baptized in the Jordan River. For a Christian to say the Holy Spirit does not dwell in him is to deny that he is a child of God, and I do not deny that I am a child of God. I am eager to tell it.
>
> I feel the Holy Spirit dwells in me at all times. Sometimes it's like a grain of mustard seed, but

it's there, and at times, like when we sing those gospel songs, I think it does shine through me. That's what happened at Las Vegas and at most of our concerts lately. The people feel that special something, and they come down front to shake my hand. That's what happened at Las Vegas.

Unfortunately, several national religious magazines picked up the inaccurate "denial" story and passed the news on to their readers that Cash had denied receiving the Holy Spirit. As is so often the case, the same magazines overlooked Cash's explanation, and to date none of them have corrected their original reports.

6

ON A WARM, SUMMER EVENING LAST YEAR, a small group of Johnny Cash's closest friends gathered in his office suite, each one unlocking and locking the door behind him again as he entered.

They were all there, all the valued friends whom Cash knows and trusts well: Carl Perkins, all the Tennessee Three, his parents, sisters Reba Hancock and Joann Yates, Larry Lee, Maybelle Carter, Jimmy Snow, and Hal Landers, a movie producer who is a friend of long-standing. They had come at Johnny's special invitation to share with him the thing which he calls "the most important piece of work I've ever done in my life."

Johnny and June came through the door to a

round of "Howdy folks, how ya doing"—he wearing an open-necked khaki shirt, she a pair of pale-blue slacks and a white cotton blouse. The guests were seated informally, scattered around the big carpeted room in chairs and on couches, facing a screen that had been pulled from the ceiling. A monstrous movie projector—one that will show a film and sound track before they have been spliced together—stood at the back of the room.

June got up to talk, and the conversation stopped. "Johnny and I want all of you to know that we really appreciate your coming here tonight." Her voice was open and bright and friendly. "We've invited you here because all of you are our very closest friends—lots of you have been for a long time. As you know, this movie is something that we've prayed about and worked on for years, and now that it's about ready, we wanted to share it with you. We feel like it's the most important thing in our lives right now. Just keep in mind that this is still a rough cut and there's some editing left to be done. But it's pretty close now, and we wanted you to see it."

The lights went down and the projector started and what it showed the small, quiet group that night is one of the most memorable pieces of film that ever lit up the silver screen since the discovery of celluloid.

The film they saw was *Gospel Road*—a feature-length documentary of the life of Christ, written, produced, narrated, and financed by Johnny Cash. Since February of 1973, thousands have seen it in theaters all across the country, and most would probably echo the reaction of a viewer at that first showing: "Man, I tell you, it's a grabber!" June Carter was not exaggerating when she called it "the most important thing in our lives."

Gospel Road had its official world premiere in Charlotte, North Carolina, on February 14, 1973. In the weeks that followed, it was released in scattered cities (Houston, Memphis, Los Angeles) at times arranged to coincide with Cash appearances. Nationwide distribution, which is being handled by Twentieth-Century Fox, began in the month of April, and by early 1974 the movie will have appeared in virtually every town of any size in the country. First refusal rights for television are held by the American Oil Company, and the projection now is that the film will appear as a TV special in late 1974 or early 1975.

Cash is a man who has a capacity for great intensity when he sets his hand to a project, and that intensity has never been greater than with the production of *Gospel Road*. He put up the money for the project himself (reportedly in the amount of $500,000) because he was determined to do it his way. "I wanted to do it the way I felt led to do it," he explained, "and if I had called in other people to finance it I would have had to let them help edit it too." Though he admittedly is taking an enormous financial risk, Cash does not seem anxious about his investment. "I've made a lot of big money, and I think God let that happen for a purpose. It's God's money anyway—He's just letting me use it to make a film about Jesus." If there are any profits from the film, they will be given to charity.

The movie tells the story of Christ's life in narration and song, with bits of dramatization woven in among the narrative and musical passages. Though Cash does not act in the film, he sings its eight new songs (which have been released on a new album by Columbia) and narrates throughout. He is a towering presence in the film, and personally provides it with the emotional wallop which it packs. Somehow, unexpectedly, it seems right and natural—Johnny Cash in the Holy Land. This huge, rough-hewn man, dressed all in black down to his soft leather boots, picking his way across the strange and craggy terrain—somehow he fits the character of the place. He walks by the side of the sea; he sits on the ugly-beautiful rocks; he stands on the top of the mountain, wind blowing his hair, and it is clear that he is at peace and at home.

Gospel Road actually began in Cash's mind several years earlier when he first toured the Holy

Land. "Even now I am drawn like a prodigal son to the land . . ." goes a line in the movie, and that must have been Cash's feeling when he first saw Palestine. He took recording equipment with him the second time he went, and taped a long-play album which bore the title "Johnny Cash in The Holy Land." "Even while I was doing that record," he remembers, "I realized that was just a drop in the bucket compared to what could be done." The idea was expanded to that of a television special to be called "In the Footsteps of Jesus," but soon even that idea seemed too small to contain Cash's vision.

"I really wanted to zero in on Christ," Cash says. "I had never seen a film on Christ that I could relate to, one that was really believable. As I got to know the Lord better, the idea really took hold on me. The original concept was that I would just walk the places Jesus walked and talk about Him. Later the idea was expanded to include dramatization and music.

"Billy Graham helped inspire that part of it. He was at our house one day and said, 'Why can't we get the really good songwriters to do some songs on Jesus that are as good as the best in the business?' And that's what we've done in the movie. Every one of these songs would stand up as a hit all by itself." (Songs for the film were written by such well-known persons as Joe South, Kris Kristofferson, John Denver, Larry Gatlin, Christopher Wren, and Cash himself.)

So Cash went to work on the script, writing it himself with the help of a friend named Larry Murray. (It comes as a surprise to many that Cash is an excellent writer; he has won several awards for his back-liner copy for record albums, and has written brilliantly in the film script.) As he wrote, Cash burrowed deeply into Scripture to learn all he could about Jesus. "I dug into the gospels every day," he recalls, "and then got into the Old Testament—Daniel, Micah, Isaiah, all the prophets. With my rededication, I began to really *know* Jesus rather than just know about Him. I began to feel Him. My life changed, and my script continued to change as I worked. That was a wonderful experience. Every day it seems like I would find something about Jesus I hadn't known before. I got so excited as I worked, sometimes I'd call Brother Snow on the phone just to tell him what I was finding out."

After six months and what Cash estimates was ten rewrite jobs, the script was completed and he was ready to start filming. His entourage, including a production crew of thirty American and Israeli technicians, spent the month of November, 1971, in Israel, working every day, all day. It was an exhausting schedule, the whole crew arising at 3:30 A.M. to travel to isolated desert locations and shoot until dark, and then work long past that. "It seemed like the Lord gave us a miracle every day," Cash says. "Shooting all that film in a month was impossible, but we got it done anyway." Large crowds followed the popular singer around the countryside, and on one occasion Cash took time out from the busy shooting schedule to be baptized by immersion in the Jordan River.

Gospel Road was directed by Bob Elfstrom, who also played the role of Christ in the film. There were many familiar faces before the cameras other than Cash himself: June Carter played the part of Mary Magdalene; Larry Lee was John the Baptist; Jimmy Snow, Pontius Pilate; and Reba Hancock, Mary the mother of Jesus. The parts of the twelve disciples were played by young people who were recruited on location by means of an ad in a Tel Aviv newspaper. From their month's work the crew got what Mrs. Hancock called "seventy hours of really good footage," then flew home to begin taping the sound track and editing the seventy hours down to the ninety minutes of finished film.

Most viewers of *Gospel Road* will be struck by the difference between the Johnny Cash of this film and the Cash that they last saw on the big screen. That was in the movie called *The Gunfight*, a Western in which he costarred with Kirk Douglas. In that film Cash played a hard-bitten gunslinger, brawling, cursing, drinking, and visiting the local prostitute. (Cash refused to allow the scene with the prostitute, played by Karen Black, to be shot as originally planned: with Miss Black in the nude.) Who would have guessed while watching Cash in that film, that when he next appeared in a movie he would be standing on a mountaintop in Israel, holding a Bible in his hand, talking about Jesus Christ?

Cash chose to unveil his new work in a fashion typical for him, presenting it to the people of Nashville in a prerelease showing that beat the Charlotte premiere by several months. On that occasion, Cash bought out the 2,020-seat Tennessee Theater, sent special invitations to members of the show business community, and threw the rest of the seats open to the public. Dozens of well-known stars were present, a huge crowd packed the house and the sidewalks outside, and the affair had all the excitement of a Hollywood opening. A local newspaper reported that the first-time showing "triggered an enthusiastic standing ovation, many leaving the theater moist-eyed and moved."

Gospel Road is an eloquent expression of an honest, somewhat unconventional view of Jesus Christ. It is the story of Jesus set to banjo and guitar rather than to violin and harp—and the result is a forceful, masculine version of a Jesus who is compelling and strong. Short work is made of the birth and childhood of Jesus; the focus is on His manhood. The script reads, "Jesus was a carpenter, and He could build a table that would hold up. . . ." That line hints at the thrust of Cash's portrayal.

"Lots of people go all their lives thinking Jesus was some kind of pious pushover," Cash says in explaining the film's approach. "He's been portrayed as a sissy, and I'm just not buying that concept of Him. He didn't bawl on that cross; I think if you or I had been up there we would've squalled and bawled and tried to get down. Not Jesus. He was a real man. He walked into the seat of authority—Him just a man of the street—and called the Pharisees hypocrites to their faces. That takes a real man too.

"God was born a human so men could relate to Him, you know? But the problem is that things have been overlooked about Him that should have been emphasized. He was a real human being with great compassion, and a special gentleness toward women and down-and-outers. This film shows Him very much as a human—like He eats boiled eggs and bread with his hands; He gets a rock in His sandal and it hurts Him—that sort of thing."

When Cash talks about Jesus, he generates a special intensity. One is gripped by the certainty that he has been greatly moved and changed by this dynamic view of a living Christ. How will the public, more accustomed to the usual bland, Pablum version of Jesus, react to this virile portrait Cash has drawn? "I don't know. I may have some criticism by people who don't understand." He pauses, then goes on with a little extra emphasis. "But I did it the way I felt led to do it, and that's the way it has to be."

Which brings to mind a statement made long before by one who knows him very well: "The only reason that Johnny Cash is controversial is that he is so genuine and honest that it constantly sets him in conflict with phonies."

7

THE PLACE IS JAM-CRAM-PACKED AND THE faithful are getting restless. They are there, three thousand of them, come from near and far to hear the man whose music says best all those things that country music says so well—to hear him sing of love and pain and dreams and the sweet sadness of days gone by. They have come to hear Johnny Cash, and they have waited long enough now, and they are getting restless.

The last of the preliminary groups is finishing up, and the crew scurries to change the stage in the brief moment that the curtain is down, frantically dragging amplifiers and tugging at microphones as the performers file onto the stage. Finally they are all in place, the Statler Brothers on one side, Maybelle Carter and the girls on the other, the Tennessee Three in the middle, and Carl Perkins out front making a last-minute check of a guitar string as the curtain goes up on the newly-populated stage.

Hidden somewhere in the darkened hall, the announcer coughs into a microphone. "Ladies and gentlemen" . . . and the drone of the audience dissipates into a hopeful hush—"It is now my pleasure to introduce without further ado" . . . a little boy slides further toward the front of his seat—"The most exciting man in American music today . . . Mr. Johnny Cash!"

And onto the stage he moves, as the sidemen settle into a rhythmic, loping beat that barely penetrates the roar of applause. His guitar is slung across his back, and he is wearing black, his high-heeled boots making him seem even taller than they remember. He is big and his frame dominates the little piece of spotlight that punches through the dark cavern to reach him. The crowd suddenly surges toward him—it is as though the sight of him has opened an invisible gate that held them in their seats, and now they crush against the stage and reach out to him with their hands and their spirits and he reaches back in quick, hard handclasps.

The darkness is shattered again, again, again,

again by the explosions of flashbulbs that burst from dozens of just-load-and-shoot cameras. And the steady, even beat of the guitars goes on and on until finally The Man steps back from the crowd, pulls a mike close to his mouth, and lets the song happen one more time. "Six foot six, he stood on the ground . . ."

After the song is finished, and the squeals and cheers and whistles have gone up and down again, he sings another and another and another, and the crowd laps up the sound like a thirsty pup under a dripping faucet. He sings of all the things they feel so deeply—and he moves as he sings, somehow graceful for all his size, as he gives himself completely to the show. Ah, it's show time, folks, complete with a little jig-step and two harmonicas and the clean, undiluted drive of that delicious sound that washes over the hall, sweeping over all that lies in its way. And he *is* exciting, oh, my goodness he is exciting!

Now June Carter steps down to join him in front, and the crowd hollers happily as she starts to sing. Their voices bounce against one another comfortably but never quite slide together. She goes at it with a verve and a wham-bang and he grins that cockeyed grin that says, "I got me some kind of woman" and the crowd sees it and loves it and wants the music to go on and on.

Later, much later, the mood is subdued and the

crowd is hushed and Johnny Cash begins to talk. That gentle-gruff voice now is naked, stripped of guitars and drums and backup chorus, and it goes out with an extra weight that comes only from him. He is saying that he is forty years old now, and that he has reached a point in his life where he wants to contribute to the things he believes in. And chief of those things is the Kingdom of God, and he wants more than anything else to do what God put him in this world to do.

Every eye stays fixed on him as he pauses, sighs that quick, hard sigh, and continues. He says that he is going to sing a gospel song, that he has sung gospel songs all his life, but that now he sings them differently than before. He says that now he feels what he is singing because his life is dedicated to the God he is singing about.

And he starts once again to sing, this time that old invitation hymn called "Supper Time." And once again the sound of his voice weaves a magic spell. But this time there are no whistles, no shouts, no flashbulbs. There is only a jam-cram-packed house of three thousand people who are listening and feeling something that can't be pressed on a record or written in a book. Vibrations from the man in black—that is what they are feeling. Vibrations that tell them he is changed, he is different. Vibrations that tell them that this giant of a man has finally grabbed hold of something bigger than he is, and that it has made a new Johnny Cash out of the old one.

It is a thrill to watch Johnny Cash perform and reflect on the marvelous way that God has led him to what he is from what he once was. But, in telling the story, it is possible to be caught up in the glamour surrounding this magnetic man and forget a basic and important point: What God did for Johnny Cash, He can do for any man.

The history of mankind for the past two thousand years is sprinkled with tales like the one just told—only the names and the details are different. The heart of the story—that a wandering, restless soul finds meaning and purpose in Christian discipleship—has happened time and time again. And it will continue to happen so long as people in need turn to God and put their trust in Him.

If your life is empty, Jesus Christ can fill it. If it is confused, He can give it direction. If it is marked by failure and weakness that makes you less than what you ought to be, He can turn it around and make it new. But first you must give it to Him, surrender it to Him, place it completely in His hands.

Some think that vibrant, exciting discipleship is only for the few—only for the talented, the rich, the glib, the well-educated, the famous. That is not true.

Every page of Scripture hammers home the same message: The grace of God is freely given to every man. Johnny Cash was wealthy and famous when he dedicated himself to God, but you can come to Him without a dime in your pocket or a friend in the world, and He will receive you just as gladly, and bless you just as richly. Giving yourself to God does not require that you be as talented as a Johnny Cash; for He can take any person of any ability and use that person for His Kingdom. You do not need to suffer the kind of tragedy and pain that Cash experienced before God will love you; He stands ready to embrace you in any circumstance, whether you are on the top or on the bottom, whether you are scarred and sinful or still a young child.

There are only two requirements. First, you must recognize that you *need* God's presence in your life. When Cash made his rededication, it would have seemed that he needed nothing. His career was flourishing; his health was strong. But he recognized that, however self-sufficient he appeared, his life was empty unless God was present in it. No man has ever come to know God without first realizing that he needs Him above all else.

Secondly, you must become personally attached to Jesus Christ. "I began to really *know* Jesus rather than just know *about* Him," Cash says, and that aptly describes the change that makes the difference. Like Cash, you can know Jesus Christ personally, so that He becomes an exciting, powerful presence in your life. And when that happens, when you come to know Him for yourself, you will experience the same newness of life that this man in black has found. And you, like him, will learn the thrill of true Christian discipleship.

Supper Time

Many years ago in days of childhood I used to play
    till evening shadows come,
Then winding down an old familiar pathway I heard
    my mother call at set of sun.

Come home, come home it's supper time,
The shadows lengthen fast;
Come home, come home it's supper time;
We're going home at last.

One day beside her bedside I was kneeling,
And angel wings were winnowing the air;
She heard the call for Supper Time in heaven,
And now I know she's waiting for me there.

Come home, come home it's supper time,
The shadows lengthen fast;
Come home, come home it's supper time;
We're going home at last.

In visions now I see her standing yonder,
And her familiar voice I hear once more;
The banquet table's ready up in heaven,
It's supper time upon the golden shore.

Come home, come home it's supper time,
The shadows lengthen fast;
Come home, come home it's supper time,
We're going home at last.